FROM SOUP TO NUTS

The Cannibal Lover's Cookbook

By OMNIVOROUS
(as told to Jon Macks)

Simon & Schuster

SIMON & SCHUSTER
Rockefeller Center
1230 Avenue of the Americas
New York, NY 10020

SIMON & SCHUSTER and colophon are registered
trademarks of Simon & Schuster, Inc.

Designed by Bonni Leon-Berman

Manufactured in the United States of America

1   3   5   7   9   10   8   6   4   2

Library of Congress Cataloging-in-Publication Data
is available.

ISBN 0-684-86984-5

Illustration on page 29 by Kevin Pope.
Photograph on page 30 courtesy of Archive Photos.
Photograph on page 69 courtesy of Archive Photos/Popperfoto.
Photograph on page 98 courtesy of Corbis/Reuters.

**To Julie, Daniel,
Samantha,
and Ricky**

CONTENTS

I never met a man I didn't like.

—Will Rogers

FROM SOUP TO NUTS

INTRODUCTION

For legal reasons, I am not permitted to tell you who I am, nor can I drop any hints as to my identity. For the purposes of this book, my name is Omnivorous. Just as Anonymous wrote a book about the world he knew best — politics — I have undertaken (if you will indulge my use of that word) a book about my beloved world, the culinary world of cannibalism.

And who is this man the world will now know as Omnivorous? I'm an educated man, a hockey and baseball fan, a collector of antiques, a bon vivant, someone whose knowledge of wine dwarfs that of the legendary Parker . . . and, yes, I'm a cannibal.

I am what the politically correct call a CBC — cannibal by choice. Unlike many of my peers, I was not forced to eat human flesh in order to survive. And unlike others of the cannibal persuasion, I joined the tribe early in life. Even at the tender age of eleven—and, trust me, eleven is when young boys are the most tender—I knew my destiny. I'll never forget, one Friday afternoon, my mother took me to a store on the Upper East Side, and while she was at the counter, she playfully accused the butcher of weighing his thumb. To my mother and the butcher, it was a joke; to me, it was a revelation. As the two of them stood there laughing, I began to think, "Why not weigh his thumb, and if it is meaty enough, why not eat it?" It looked tasty. I had been reading Freud at the time and if the master was right in his theory that all men secretly want to suck their thumbs, I wanted to know, what's wrong with eating one?

Those of the Hebrew faith announce at their bar mitzvah, "Today I am a man"; from that moment in the butcher shop, I could honestly say, "Today I am a cannibal."

But I have never been content to selfishly hoard my wisdom. Like many a convert, I want to proselytize, to share my knowledge, to show others that the key to a full and happy life is eating well. It's true—in my own small way, I have always wanted to serve man; the logical way to do this was to write a book.

Since my escape from some unenlightened yet protein-rich jailkeepers at a correctional institution in 1995 (and, yes, gentle reader, I have deliberately altered dates and the first and last names of my meals in order to keep the authorities from tracking my whereabouts and revealing my identity), I have been circling the globe, writing and thinking, tasting and sampling some of the best food in the world. I've dined with royalty in the Netherlands and on royalty in Thailand; chewed the fat with the indigenous people of Peru; gone back for seconds in China, the world's largest buffet; and visited England, where the only meat worth eating is walking on two legs. In every land, I took notes, tasted the local cuisine, and started to put together the outline for this, my gift to you.

For I want to do more than share my recipes with you. I want you to share my way of thinking, because to me, cannibalism, like the Junior League, is more than a lifestyle, it's a way of life. So as you peruse this tome, earmarking the pages with interesting recipes, I urge you to keep in mind the Golden Rule of Cannibalism: as Hannibal Lecter would say, in an uncivilized age, there is nothing more civilized than having a few friends for dinner.

— "Omnivorous," CBC

1

A BRIEF HISTORY OF CANNIBALISM

Cannibalism, n.: the practice of those who eat their own kind.

Current slang for cannibalism: man munching; slurping the *sapiens;* doing the body-cavity search and snack; the full Dahmer; Tysonizing; the stalk, stab, and slurp; eating out; Donner dining.

Anthropologists believe that the first recorded act of cannibalism occurred in the South of France in approximately 9500 B.C. I have often thought that B.C. should stand for "before cannibalism," but at present, my suggestions to the calendar people have gone unanswered. A series of stick figure drawings in the Lascaux caves pictures a family of five, emaciated, staring at empty food bowls and afraid to leave their cave to hunt because of a sabertooth tiger lurking outside. The next series of drawings pictures a happy family of four, with full bellies, and in the corner, near the illustrator's symbol, are the bones of the smallest member of the cave family.

Since that moment some 11,500 years ago, which not only is the first recorded act of cannibalism but also marks the dawn of gourmet French dining, there have been many great cannibal moments. At the risk of showing off my vast knowledge of history, before setting the table, let us take a moment to study those who have come before us.

THE FIVE GREATEST MOMENTS IN CANNIBAL HISTORY

(as voted by a panel of cannibal chefs, historians, and fans)

 THE URUGUAY RUGBY TEAM PLANE CRASH OF 1972

This not only became the inspiration for two movies, it introduced the concept of gourmet airline food.

2. THE DONNER PARTY, FEBRUARY 1847

America's first recorded acts of cannibalism. The Donner Party, stranded in the Sierra Nevadas, stayed alive by eating the flesh of the deceased. Despite claims by Clarence Birdseye, many consider this to also mark the invention of frozen food.

3. ALFERD PACKER

Just as Edison's lightbulb was the result of a mistake in the lab, just as the invention of the Post-it Note was the result of a chemist's failure to invent a supersticky glue, the discovery of Rocky Mountain oysters came about because of a colossal miscalculation by Alferd Packer. Rather than wait until July for a trek through the Rockies, Alferd accidentally or hungrily left Salt Lake City with five gold prospectors in February of 1874. Two months later, Alferd Packer arrived alone in Gunnison, Colorado, packing his five friends' cash, clothes, and thirty extra pounds.

A little-known fact: Alferd had tremors in his hands; thus, he is credited with being the inventor of Shake 'n Bake.

> AUTHOR'S NOTE: I find it fascinating that so many of the great moments in cannibal history involve snow. The Andes Mountains, the Sierras, the Rockies, the siege of Leningrad. I guess cold weather brings out the appetite in—and for—people.

4 RICHARD PARKER, JULY 25, 1884

If it were not for Richard Parker, cruise passengers would not have the twenty-four-hour gourmet dining they enjoy on the Princess, Norwegian, and Royal Caribbean lines. Richard was the English cabin boy from the SS *Mignonette* who became a five-course meal for three hungry cannibals adrift in a lifeboat for nineteen days in the South Atlantic.

Apparently, they had no qualms about eating him because they were English. Those bastards will even eat boiled mutton.

5 JEFFREY DAHMER

If Wolfgang Puck is considered the founder of California nouveau cuisine, then Jeffrey Dahmer deserves credit as the man who revitalized cannibal cooking. One of the many negative aspects of the sixties "Make love not war" anti-Vietnam philosophy was the backlash against killing and eating people. Vegetarianism was in, eating beef was out, and chowing down on human beef was even worse. To illustrate, think of what happened to the music group the Buoys. Do you remember their hit song "Timothy"? It was a great song based on the Richard Parker story, transferred to a coal mine, which described in loving detail the cannibalizing of Timothy. Just a beautiful song. But did the peace freaks in the music industry let the Buoys ever record another song? Have you seen them in concert? Do you even see them on a VH1 *Where Are They Now?* special. I think not. They disappeared from view as if they had been eaten alive.

In short, if it were not for Jeffrey Dahmer and his wacky Wisconsin love life, cannibalism would never have re-emerged in the American mainstream. Thank God those midwesterners love their beef.

THE FIVE WORST MOMENTS IN CANNIBAL HISTORY

1 JEFFREY DAHMER
Jeffrey makes this list, too. What kind of cook lets his meat develop freezer burn?

2 MIKE TYSON
I think Mike Tyson is crazy. Not for biting Evander Holyfield's ear. For spitting it out.

3 MARV ALBERT
Did Marv have the perfect chance to make a great meal out of that Virginia woman? Yesss! Did he do anything more than leave evidence on her back? Nooo! What, was he on a diet? To me, that is more embarrassing than the fact that a nice Jewish boy wears a pink dress, high heels and bad toupee.

4 DR. KEVORKIAN
The man has assisted in 130 suicides but all he does is take the bodies to a motel room and call the police. Doesn't he know there are starving people in Kosovo?

5 JOHN WAYNE GACY
The man kills thirty-three people and leaves them under the porch uneaten. What a clown!

A WORD ABOUT ANDREI CHIKATILO

Cannibal fans have been arguing over Andrei since his arrest in 1990. Is Andrei a cannibal or just a serial killer? As Bill James would say about baseball players, first let's look at the record, then look at what his peers said about him. He was responsible for fifty-two killings, and in almost every instance his victims' necks were bitten and sex organs were mutilated and munched on. But did he actually enjoy eating them? Did he take the time to prepare and present his food? Did he ever share his table with cannibal friends? In every case, the answer is no. He killed and ate out of anger, not out of the love of food. Moreover, those who knew him best, the people of the Ukraine, refer to him in every newspaper report as the "Shelter Belt Killer," not the "Shelter Belt Cannibal." In short, the man is no cannibal, he is just fond of giving fatal hickeys.

But this is not a history text, nor is it an anthropology treatise; it is a cookbook and a celebration of a joyous way of life. So rather than explore the cannibal cultures of the past and present with text, let us understand them the way God intended—through their recipes. But before dismembering and dining, we must prepare.

2

PREPARING
TO COOK

I find that two things can ruin a great dinner: first is an obnoxious, uninformed dinner companion; second is a chewy dinner companion. Which brings us to Omnivorous's First Rule of Cannibal Cuisine—always use fresh ingredients.

Gentle reader, it is my intent to spare you years of trial and error, to share with you the wisdom I have learned from hundreds of mistakes. So many novice cannibals select victims at random, bash them with a mallet, drive hundreds of miles with their meal in the trunk of a hot car to a deserted campsite, hack off a few body parts, cook over a small fire, and complain later of indigestion. What do they expect? Would they blindly grab a chicken breast from the butcher's counter without first looking for discoloration, would they transport fish in the hot trunk of their car without ice, would they cook a turkey sans proper basting? I think not. So is your next-door neighbor Bob worth any less special treatment than a porterhouse steak? Again, I think not.

CHOOSING THE MENU

There are so many places to find the right type of meat: conventions, dating services, church, train depots. Personally, I have always favored the use of door-to-door salesmen. They have three key advantages: first of all, the food comes to you, fresh and at the proper 98.6 degrees; second, because these nomads of the business world keep odd schedules, it is easy to disavow any knowledge that they ever visited your house (let's see: blue suit, brown shoes, carrying an Amway sales kit—sorry, Officer, I don't recall him); third, and I hope the PC police don't jump all over this, it's not like the world really needs door-to-door salespeople.

CHOOSING THE RIGHT CUT OF MEAT

Once you have a fresh selection of meats to choose from, how do you pick the right one? The same way your mother would—by sight, smell, and touch.

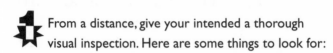 From a distance, give your intended a thorough visual inspection. Here are some things to look for:

LIVER SPOTS—If it's discolored on the outside, it won't be pink and tender after cooking. This explains why no one has eaten Katharine Hepburn in ninety-three years.

EXCESSIVE BODY HAIR—Spend hours on the meal, not on shaving and plucking Stanley Tucci's forearms. Or any woman from France.

FAT—Hair and liver spots are bad, fat is good. You're looking for a relatively high body fat percentage, anywhere from 25 to 30 percent. Unlike a fillet under cellophane, you won't be able to tell if there is sufficient marbleized fat. So look for a good, consistent body fat distribution, a slight jiggle in the upper arms and thighs when your prospective meal is walking. When in doubt, look for a man whose pants size is larger than his age.

2 Once you've predetermined your selection, employ your sense of smell. Never choose anyone who wears too much cologne or perfume. These artificial chemicals will ruin even the finest cuts of meat. Would you eat chicken that's been marinating in English Leather since 1967? I think not. But now I'm going to go against the conventional wisdom. For years, the great cannibal chefs of Europe have held to the theory that people who sweat are a poor cut of meat. Wrong, wrong, wrong. Think of it this way: What could be more tender than a fillet of your fellow man that has been stewing in its own juices for weeks?

3 You've eyeballed your victim, gotten close enough to inhale his bouquet, now comes the final use of your God-given senses—the sense of touch. Depending on the social situation and your degree of familiarity with the meal, shake hands, put your hand on his shoulder, hug him, pat him on the back. With each touch, you are looking for the same thing—ripeness and firmness.

OMNIVOROUS'S WARNING—Use a Light Touch. Remember, You Want a Meal, Not a Sexual Harassment Lawsuit

A special word about plumbers. In all my years as a cannibal, I have found that for everyday dining, there is nothing better to eat than a plumber. Those low-slung pants allow you to select a good rump roast, every plumber is at least 60 percent marbleized fat, and there is no danger of too much cologne and deodorant on a man working in the same sweaty uniform for weeks. To me, plumbers truly are the other white meat.

The Prime Cuts of Meat

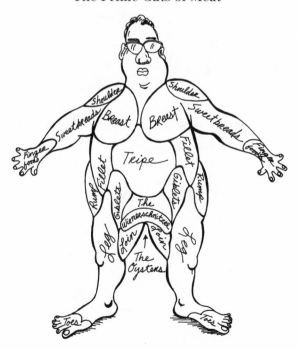

A WORD ABOUT DRY-AGED BEEF

Dry-ageing beef is the technique of preparing a prime cut of meat by letting it age in a dry refrigerator for five to six weeks. The wait is well worth it. Steak lovers know that dry-aged beef is simply the most tender, smoky morsel one can put in the oral cavity. The masters of this were the great Italian chefs of the 1940s.

UTENSILS

Beethoven did not conduct his Ninth Symphony without a woodwind section, the Rothschilds do not prepare their grapes without a winepress, and a cannibal chef does not cook without the proper utensils. Assuming your kitchen has the basics, here are the specialty items you'll need.

Kosher salt
At least five types of saucepans
1 baseball bat for meat tenderizing (I recommend the Easton Z-Core, 32-inch, 27-ounce. Some prefer the heavier 34-inch, 29-ounce Redline, but to me the key is bat speed. If a 32-ounce bat is good enough for Tony Gwynn, it's good enough for you.)
1 electric hacksaw
The world's largest industrial-size Cuisinart
1 2-gallon pot
1 70-gallon pot
Janitor drums for discarding unused body parts. Today's modern homes have those cheap garbage disposals, and a femur can cost you a $500 plumber's bill. And woodchippers leave too much forensic evidence.
Hefty trash bags and dry ice (you'll want to save the giblets and major bones to prepare homemade stock)
200 gallons club soda (great for removing bloodstains)
1 spice rack
1 regular rack
1 industrial-size oven

OMNIVOROUS'S RULE OF THUMB: There is nothing more important for a cannibal chef to do than wash his hands. Once I ate a pair of unwashed hands and ended up in bed for two weeks.

3

MY FAVORITE RECIPES— FROM SOUP TO NUTS

SOUPS AND STEWS

Chicken soup may be good for the soul but *Homo sapiens* soup is good for the appetite. Never think of your victim's bones, intestines, and unused body parts as evidence to be incinerated—think of them as the makings of a great soup. Too many Americans think soup means opening a can of Camp-

bell's. To a cannibal, the best soup Monsieur Campbell could have ever made is if he had killed those annoying "M'm! M'm! Good!" Campbell twins and made
a consommé.

As Emeril Lagasse has said, the key to great soup is
great stock. But his words of caution about his soup
hold true for ours: You cannot expect to clean out the
meat locker, throw some entrails into a pot, and expect good results. As always, each soup or stew re-
quires the freshest ingredients. And there is so much
to choose from. Heinz may think there are fifty-seven
varieties, but cannibals know there are six billion varieties.

Menestrone

Serves 4

Although most people enjoy minestrone as a hot first course, in the summer, it can be served at room temperature. This recipe is the classic from the chefs of Little Italy who perfected their skills in the 1920s. Little Italy is one of the many reasons I love the Big Apple—for not only is New York the melting pot for people from all around the world, it's also a great place to melt some people in your cooking pot.

2 men
8 cups homemade beef stock
3 cups shredded cabbage
1 can tomato paste
1 cup kidney beans . . . or 1 kidney
1 potato with eyes
4 tomatoes

Cook the men in a large soup pot. Add the beef stock, cabbage, and tomato paste. Bring to a boil.

Reduce the heat, add the kidney, potatoes, and tomatoes. Simmer for 10 minutes. Serve with Parmesan cheese.

OMNIVOROUS'S HELPFUL HINT: Kidneys obtained from a dialysis center are clean and leave no bitter aftertaste.

THE CANNIBAL LOVER'S COOKBOOK

Gum-bo

Makes 12 first-course servings or 8 main-course servings

Longtime friends in the Big Easy have come to blows over the question "Whose mama makes the best gumbo?" To a cannibal, the answer is easy—it's the mama with the best gums.

1 cup oil or sweat
1 cup onions
2 cups peppers
2 quarts homemade stock
okra, filé powder, Tabasco
1 cup oysters—either type
24 to 36 gums and lips (depending on size)
4 cups long-grained rice

Heat the oil in a large pot. Add onions and peppers and sauté. Stir in the stock. Add spices to taste. Add oysters, gums, and lips. Simmer for 30 minutes. Serve with ¹/₃ cup rice.

OMNIVOROUS'S HELPFUL HINT: You can find the best ingredients for gumbo by staking out the local pharmacy. The people buying dental floss and tartar-control Listerine will, as a general rule, be free of gingivitis and have the healthiest gums.

OMNIVOROUS'S HELPFUL HINT #2: Never use the lips and gums of people from LA. Collagen can ruin many a fine gumbo.

Caribbean Soup

Serves 4

What makes this soup so tasty and has your guests coming back for more is the addition of 1 ounce of fine Jamaican ganga. True, it is illegal, but the ganga is going to be a lot easier to explain than the five severed heads in your meat locker. What is the district attorney going to do, give you life in prison plus a $100 fine for illegal possession? I think not.

4 cups homemade stock
2 cups coconut milk
2 serrano chiles
1 clove garlic
1 nutmeg
1 tablespoon cornstarch (easily obtained from corns or bunions)
2 boat people (if they're good enough for sharks, they're good enough for your table)
1 pound butternut squash
1 ounce ganga

Heat the homemade stock and coconut milk, stirring in the chiles, garlic, and nutmeg. Stir in cornstarch to thicken.

Put the boat people in the Cuisinart and puree them; stir into the soup. Add the butternut squash.

Serve cold with ganga sprinkled on the top.

OMNIVOROUS'S HELPFUL HINT: If you're feeling under the weather, remember that soup has always been known for its medicinal effect. Under California's Proposition 215, so is marijuana. And under Pat Buchanan's interpretation of California's Proposition 187, I believe it is permissible to kill and eat an illegal Caribbean immigrant.

Stew

Serves 1 for a month

What do you do when you catch a victim and find, much to your dismay, that he's tough and chewy? Do you toss him in a dumpster like a New Jersey prom baby? I think not. Cannibals have too much respect for the value of human life to ever do such a thing. The solution is simple—turn him into stew.

Some guy named or renamed Stew
1 potato
3 cups homemade beef stock
1 cup chopped onions
1 can tomato paste
Flour
3 cups of any 1977 California Pinot Noir (it was a very bad year)

Dice the Stew meat into cubes. Brown. Remove the eyes from the potato. Leave the eyes in Stew. Combine the potatoes and Stew.

Stir the Stew into a large pot with the beef stock. Add chopped onions, tomato paste, and flour. Add the wine as you simmer. Serve.

OMNIVOROUS'S HELPFUL HINT: What happens when even you cannot stomach another day of Stew? Do what I do. Every Thanksgiving and Christmas, I go into the freezer, take out all the leftovers from the past year, throw them into a giant pot, make 100 gallons of stew and feed the homeless. Not only are you doing a good deed but, cleaned up and fed, today's homeless person is tomorrow's entrée.

APPETIZERS AND HORS D'OEUVRES

Nothing starts a meal off better than finger food. Or toe food. For those listening to this on "books on tape," that is "toe food," not "tofu." In fact, any of the body's extremities are great to munch on, whether before dinner, while enjoying any of the first-growth Bordeaux from 1945, or while watching a Three Tenors concert on PBS.

Remember, with appetizers and hors d'oeuvres, less goes a long, long way.

Chicken Fingers

Serves 5

Are the chicken fingers you get in a restaurant really "fingers"? For that matter, are they really even chicken? At least with this recipe, you get 100 percent real fingers. Like Lay's potato chips. I have never found anyone who could eat just one, so you will need to find a source for a large number of fingers. I have found three. (1) The nation of Iran. Ever since the Ayatollah took over in 1979, fundamentalists have amputated the hands of five thousand petty thieves and shoplifters a year. My supplier flash-freezes the hands and FedExes them to my mail drop within forty-eight hours. (2) The dumpsters outside industrial sites. Sheet-metal factories, steel mills, ironworks—anywhere there are sharp cutting edges and a disproportionate number of industrial accidents is an excellent source of delicious digits. I find OSHA to be an excellent source of locations that have the worst or, in our case, the best track record. (3) Your own meat locker: As a cannibal, you are killing and eating anywhere from twenty-five to thirty people a year. That's a minimum of 125 fingers. Remember the adage: Waste not, want not. Immediately after capturing a meal, remove the fingers and flash-freeze them in liquid nitrogen. But be careful—we don't want them to get frostbite!

20 fingers
1 egg
2 cups flour
1 cup bread crumbs
Salt and pepper
2 tablespoons paprika
3 cups corn oil

Debone the fingers. Note: My friend Martha Stewart tells me the bones make wonderful wind chimes.

Dip the fingers in egg, flour, bread crumbs, salt, pepper, and paprika. Coat and shake off excess.

Heat the oil in a Fry Daddy to 375 degrees. Fry until golden and crisp. Serve in a finger bowl.

OMNIVOROUS'S HELPFUL HINT: Just for fun, serve them in mittens.

OMNIVOROUS'S HELPFUL HINT #2: Repeat after me—always wash your hands.

Kick-Ass Chilean Con Carne

Serves 14

For those unfamiliar with Romance languages, *chile con carne* simply means a dish featuring chile powder and meat. For those unfamiliar with the colloquialism "kick-ass," it means "strong." For those unfamiliar with cannibalism, *carne* means people, and "kick-ass" is a way of tenderizing the *carne*'s buttocks. I first had this appetizer while working as a gaucho on a Chilean S&M dude ranch. At the end of the summer-long roundup, the sadists would lasso the masochists into the corral, whip their buttocks with a cat-o'-nine-tails, and brand them. I suggested adding a kicking to the whipping and thus was born the dish of "kick-ass chile."

3 tablespoons olive oil
3 large onions
5 cloves of garlic
1 chopped spleen
5 pounds of a young gaucho
2 cups canned tomatoes
2 green peppers
2 teaspoons cayenne
3 ounces Tabasco sauce
$1/2$ cup chile powder

Heat the olive oil in a large skillet, add onions and garlic, and sauté until golden brown.

Remove the spleen of your hog-tied gaucho, kicking him in the buttocks just as he expires.

Chop his spleen in a blender, fillet 5 pounds of buttock, brown, then add onions, garlic, and all other ingredients in a large saucepan. Simmer for 3 hours.

OMNIVOROUS'S HELPFUL HINT: Most people are right-handed. This means when writing at a desk, more pressure is put on the right buttock, making it more muscular and tough to chew. The left buttock, more supple and marbleized, will be tastier. Unless you know whether the victim is left- or right-handed, always use the left buttock for filleting.

Spanish Meatballs

Serves 36

I got this idea from watching the movie *Zorro*. Remember that great scene in which the Capitán shows Antonio Banderas the severed head of his brother that he keeps as a memento in a jar? Remember the next scene in which Antonio sips some of the pickled juice from the jar? Did you know why Antonio was able to pull off that scene? Because he has seen something even more wrinkled and preserved—the naked body of Melanie Griffith.

Pickle the head of your victim in a jar. Not to eat. It just makes a lovely table decoration. For the recipe, you need a strong young cabin boy.

2 tablespoons butter
2 tablespoons minced onion
1 cup bread crumbs
2 cups milk
1 egg
Salt and pepper
1 19-year-old cabin boy from a Spanish freighter
2 cups flour
1 cup cream or evaporated milk

In a large skillet, melt the butter and sauté the onion until golden brown.

Soak the bread crumbs in the milk. Add egg, onion, salt and pepper. Use a melon scooper to remove the deltoid muscles from your Spanish sailor.

Mix thoroughly. Brown the Spanish meatballs over medium heat.

Combine the flour with the cream and stir into the pan juices.

Pour the gravy over the now-brown Spanish meatballs, and serve.

OMNIVOROUS'S HELPFUL HINT: It doesn't have to be Spanish or even a sailor. Just as long as he or she is not from Scandinavia. There's something about the midnight sun that ruins their flavor.

OMNIVOROUS'S HELPFUL HINT #2: And why do we not eat the head of the sailor? Because the brains in Spain taste mainly rather plain.

Pâté de "Foie Gras" with Caramelized Plum Crostini

Serves 12

One of the most memorable evenings of my life was at a charity event I sponsored for the Juvenile Diabetes Foundation. I admit I had selfish reasons for curing diabetes—it makes the meat too sweet. The event was a $1,000-per-person wine party featuring a vertical tasting of my favorite French wine. My guests enjoyed the wine and what they thought was the best goose liver they ever tasted. I would never do that to a goose.

1/2 tablespoon unsalted butter
2 ripe red plums, sliced into 1/4 inch pieces
1 tablespoon sugar
8 ounces liver from a corpulent male
24 simple crostini

Over medium heat, melt the butter and add the plums. Sprinkle with sugar until the plums caramelize. Transfer the plums to a dish. Place a large skillet over medium heat. Take the victim's liver, sliced 1/4 inch thick, and sear.

Transfer to the crostini and top with 2 plum slices.

OMNIVOROUS'S HELPFUL HINT: Wash the liver while it is still pulsating. While washing, remove all traces of hepatitis A or B. Leave hepatitis C. It adds flavor.

Pinkies in a Blanket

Serves 3

You may ask, "Why would Omnivorous give us a recipe that serves three?" Because there are times when you have six people at your house and decide on the spur of the moment to kill three. Hasn't everyone done that at some point in their life? Just decided midway through a social event that half the guests are total bores? Some people feign illness and leave. But a cannibal knows that a boring party is an opportunity for a great meal.

The key to this dish is to surprise the victims from behind. If they start flailing wildly and punching, they could break their pinkies.

6 pinkie fingers
6 rolls

Sever and debone the pinkies. Place in a small roll or biscuit. Bake at 350 degrees for 20 minutes.

OMNIVOROUS'S HELPFUL HINT: In a pinch, you can always turn this recipe into cocktail wieners.

OMNIVOROUS'S HELPFUL HINT #2: Remember to wash those hands . . . and, in the immortal words of Marlon Brando from Last Tango in Paris, clip those fingernails.

Two Thumbs Up Academy Award Night Snack

Serves 30 to 40

In the years before I became famous, I would spend the evening of the Academy Awards hosting a black tie party at my mansion for 30 to 40 people. We would drink champagne, eat hors d'oeuvres, and watch the show. And what better snack to enjoy while watching the movies than a tribute to my favorite critics—Roger Ebert (enough to feed the nation of Latvia) and the late Gene Siskel. Think of this appetizer as movie popcorn, only with thumbs.

60 thumbs
Melted butter
Oil
Salt

Take the thumbs, put them in an Orville Redenbacher popcorn maker. Melt the butter. When the thumbs are popped, cover with oil, lightly salt, and serve.

OMNIVOROUS'S HELPFUL HINT: A good rule of thumb is 2 thumbs per guest.

OMNIVOROUS'S HELPFUL HINT #2: Your local loan shark and his delinquent customers are an excellent source of thumbs. But be clear, you don't want them broken.

THE CANNIBAL LOVER'S COOKBOOK

Buffalo Bill "Potato" Skins

Serves 2

I got the idea for this recipe reading the book *The Silence of the Lambs*. The character nicknamed Buffalo Bill was an excellent tailor who would remove the skins from his victims. He thought skins were for wearing. How unenlightened.

30 inches of skin
Salt, pepper, and paprika
Sour cream and chives

Skin the victim, using a small incision above the kidneys and slicing upward. Peel the outer epidermis off the body. Soak in an aquarium in a vegetable extract. Season with salt, pepper, and paprika.

Slice into 1-inch strips and pop into the Fry Daddy until golden brown. Serve with chives and sour cream.

OMNIVOROUS'S HELPFUL HINT: If you keep a kosher house, a good source of skins is a *mohel*.

Quiche Lorraine

Serves 10

I have always found it odd that this traditional French pie has never truly caught on with American cannibals. It is either the result of America's cholesterol-phobia or the lack of victims named Lorraine.

Pastry for a 1-crust 9-inch pie
4 strips bacon from someone named Lorraine
1 onion, thinly sliced
1 cup cubed Gruyère cheese
4 eggs, lightly beaten
2 cups cream
1 teaspoon nutmeg

Preheat oven to 450 degrees. Line the pie plate with pastry and bake 5 minutes. Cook the bacon until crisp. Cook the onion until transparent. Sprinkle the bacon, cheese, and onion over the pastry.

Combine eggs, cream, and nutmeg and strain over the onion-cheese mixture. Bake the pie for 15 minutes and serve.

OMNIVOROUS'S HELPFUL HINT: I've tried this dish with Cindys, Juanitas, and Freds. For whatever reason, it only works with someone named Lorraine.

Muscles

Serves 4

Do you like muscles as much as I do? Then head to a bodybuilding convention, lure a young bodybuilder into your van with the promise of free steroids, chloroform him, serrate his deltoids and pecs, put them on ice, and you're 90 percent of the way to having a refreshing appetizer.

1 20-pound bag of ice
Beer
20 small muscles
Cocktail sauce

Ice up the beer, ice up the muscles, dip in cocktail sauce, and enjoy.

OMNIVOROUS'S HELPFUL HINT: To avoid a bitter aftertaste, rinse any the tanning oil from the bodybuilder before eating.

Ear of Evander

Serves 2

Mike Tyson: former heavyweight champ, current fool. Only an idiot would bite off nature's most exquisite-tasting part of the human body, the truffle of the human anatomy, and spit it out. No wonder it took that MGM security guard forty-five minutes to get the remnants to the hospital. He couldn't decide whether to reattach it or swallow it.

Then again, who can really blame Mike for not trying to keep it—he would have had to give 50 percent to Don King.

1 earlobe
Ice
Ranch dressing

Carrying a small container of ice, walk up behind someone and bite their ear off. Spit the bite-size piece onto the ice and run away. Serve crispy cold with ranch dressing.

OMNIVOROUS'S HELPFUL HINT: You might want to soak the ear for 30 seconds in hydrogen peroxide to clean out the wax. A product called Hawaiian Tropic Swimmer's Ear is also effective.

OMNIVOROUS'S HELPFUL HINT #2: One of Ross Perot's ears could have ended the 1992 famine in Somalia.

MAIN COURSES

Think for a moment about your noncannibal friends. They go to dinner, they try what is considered an exotic meat, they describe it to you the next day, and the best they can come up with is that it "tastes like chicken." There are few guarantees in life or in death, but I can guarantee this one thing—there is no danger that any of these dishes will ever taste like chicken.

Fillet of Sole Wrapped in Spinach

Serves 1

It's sad to say that even in this time of plenty, people are starving. And when people are starving, it means less availability of the prime cuts of meat. But that does not mean that you as a cannibal need go without. *Au contraire.* Some of the most elegant dishes can be found at your feet. Literally.

1 sole, preferably size 10D
½ tablespoon butter
Kosher salt and black pepper
1 large, washed spinach leaf
1 lemon wedge

Thoroughly wash the sole. (Remember, there is nothing worse than getting toe fungus of the mouth.) Dot the sole with butter. Sprinkle with salt and pepper. Steam the fillet of sole for 5 to 7 minutes.

Wrap the sole in the spinach leaf, steam 2 more minutes, serve with lemon wedge.

OMNIVOROUS'S HELPFUL HINT: A close friend of mine is a practicing psychiatrist and he showed me the case files of three of his patients with a foot fetish. Stay away from the sole of anyone with that proclivity. You can't even imagine where that foot has been. They are sick sick sick!

OMNIVOROUS'S HELPFUL HINT #2: After dinner, I recommend watching Daniel Day-Lewis in his Oscar-winning performance in *My Left Foot.*

OMNIVOROUS'S HELPFUL HINT #3: Don't throw out those toes. They make a wonderful garnish or are great to munch on by the pool. But don't take my word for it, ask Fergie.

Shish Kabob

Serves 8

This summer favorite is easy to prepare, very tasty, and delightful when served with a 1992 Dusi Vineyard Peachy Canyon Zinfandel. The vegetables can vary—onions, bell peppers, tomatoes—but one essential remains the same: someone named Bob.

4 large tomatoes
2 green peppers
2 red peppers
4 onions
4 pounds of Bob
16 skewers

Slice the tomatoes, peppers, and onions into small chunks. Remove 4 pounds of meat from the flank of Bob. Dice the meat into 1-inch cubes.

Take the skewers and alternate pieces of Bob with the vegetables. The ratio should be 2 pieces of vegetable for 1 piece of Bob.

OMNIVOROUS'S HELPFUL HINT: Never let food go to waste. If it's a warm summer night, get a large tub and play one of my favorite party games—bobbing for Bob.

THE CANNIBAL LOVER'S COOKBOOK

Chuck Steak au Poivre

Serves 2

Steak lovers can argue for hours about the relative merits of the strip steak versus the porterhouse. To me, there is not a better cut of meat than a properly tenderized chuck steak. Since guys named Chuck—aka Charles—tend to be tough—Chuck Heston, Chuck Colson, Chuck Bednarik all come to mind—this dish will take some preparation, but in the end, it's well worth it. The most important part of this recipe is tenderizing the meat. After capturing a victim named Chuck, hang him by his heels in the basement. This will be a problem for LA cannibals since so few homes actually have basements. Take your trusty 32-inch, 27-ounce Easton Z-Core and tenderize the Chuck. Remember to step, pivot, and extend to get maximum bat speed. Cannibal fans of Charlie Lau will prefer to drop the top hand, but that is not my field of expertise. After tenderizing Chuck, remove 2 pounds of steak from the upper back.

2 pounds Chuck
4 teaspoons green peppercorns
2 teaspoons black peppercorns
1 tablespoon unsalted butter
4 tablespoons cognac
1/4 cup meat stock
1/4 cup heavy whipping cream

Using your bat, pound the steak until flat. Press some of the peppercorns onto each side of the steak until completely coated. Melt the butter in a medium skillet and sauté Chuck until he is brown, 2 minutes per side. Take some excess fat from Chuck, put it in the skillet, add the cognac, light it, and flame the steaks.

Add the beef stock, cream, and remaining peppercorns, mix, pour over the steaks, and serve.

OMNIVOROUS'S HELPFUL HINT: South of the border, you can use someone named Carlos.

Sweetbreads and Artichokes on Toast

Serves 4

Sweetbreads must be handled with care. After removal. Before removal, you can torture the packaging to your heart's content. Take your victim to church and, in the third pew, pierce the heart with a six-inch stiletto. Using a counterclockwise motion, slice and remove the thymus and the pancreas. You can select other internal organs to taste, but make sure you get the thymus and pancreas. Some people prefer serving this over the still-beating heart of the victim. Call me old-fashioned, but I prefer using artichoke hearts.

1 pound sweetbreads
1 tablespoon olive oil
1 tablespoon unsalted butter
¾ cup 1971 Kurt Darting Riesling
1 cup artichoke hearts

Bring a saucepan of water to a boil, add the sweetbreads, simmer 5 minutes, remove and then trim away the membranes. Save the membranes for a late-night snack. Slice the sweetbreads, heat the oil and butter in a large skillet, sauté until golden brown.

Add wine and beef stock and artichoke hearts to the skillet and stir. Serve on toasted brioche.

OMNIVOROUS'S HELPFUL HINT: Of course I was kidding about the artichoke hearts. What do I look like, a vegan?

Sweet and Sour Tongue

Serves 6

I first tasted tongue when a young man misinterpreted my interest in the Judy Garland record he was carrying as an invitation for a French kiss. I bit his tongue off so fast he makes James Brady sound like James Earl Jones. Still, the texture of that succulent flesh tartare led me to scour the world for a better way to prepare one of the world's great delicacies. This is the recipe I recommend.

4 pounds tongue (from 6 adults or Gene Simmons)
1 teaspoon balsamic vinegar
1 teaspoon cinnamon
3 cloves garlic
1 teaspoon ginger
1 cup red wine, preferably an Au Bon Climat Pinot (1996 is good, 1995 is better)

Clean the tongue under cold water. Slowly bring it to a boil, cover, and simmer 3 hours.

In a heavy saucepan, combine vinegar, cinnamon, garlic, and ginger; simmer.

Preheat oven to 325 degrees. With a paring knife, remove the stringy things at the back of the tongue, cut it in slices, spoon in sauce, and bake until bubbling.

Pour wine over the tongue to restore the natural pink color.

OMNIVOROUS'S HELPFUL HINT: The more taste buds in the tongue, the tastier it will be.

OMNIVOROUS'S HELPFUL HINT #2: Stay away from members of Congress—they tend to have forked tongues.

Sautéed Liver with Caramelized Onions

Serves 6

Why do I recommend so many liver dishes? Because it is the food of the gods. Why do I eat human liver? Because it is there.

8 ounces bacon or the love handles of a failed Weight Watcher
2 large onions
2 pounds liver

Sauté the fat of the bacon and the onions in a large skillet. Add the liver and cook until golden brown, for about 25 minutes. Serve.

OMNIVOROUS'S HELPFUL HINT: Liver makes a tasty picnic sandwich, especially if you are lucky enough to obtain the pickled liver of a George Jones or a Boris Yeltsin.

Liver with Fava Beans

Serves 1

Perhaps the most famous cannibal dish of all time is Hannibal Lecter's liver with fava beans. He recommended eating the liver of a census taker, but that would mean you can only enjoy it every ten years. But if you insist, some good news—the next census is just a few months away.

1 liver
1/2 cup milk
1/2 cup flour
Salt and pepper
2 cups fava beans

Cut the still-pulsating liver into 1-inch strips. Soak in milk for 20 minutes. Season the flour with salt and pepper; coat the liver strips. Sauté the liver in a large skillet for 5 minutes on each side. Serve over fava beans with a 1990 Opus.

OMNIVOROUS'S HELPFUL HINT: If you're eating the liver of an alcoholic, go easy on the wine with dinner.

Roasted Leg of Lucy with Garlic Guava Glaze

Serves 4

The female *Homo sapiens* is often heard to complain that the male is obsessed with breasts. It is true that some men love breasts; however, all my life, I have loved long, long legs. Especially with a garlic-guava glaze.

1 pair of legs
Kosher salt
6 garlic cloves
1 3-pound jar guava jelly

Preheat the oven to 350 degrees. Rub the legs with kosher salt.

Slit the skin and stuff with garlic slivers. Roast for 90 minutes, basting with guava jelly. Let cool 15 minutes before carving.

OMNIVOROUS'S HELPFUL HINT: With two legs, there will be plenty of leftovers and some of your dinner guests may be too shy to ask for Saran Wrap to take some home. That is why a thoughtful host will always volunteer a "people bag."

OMNIVOROUS'S HELPFUL HINT #2: If your entrée is a European woman, for God's sake, wax her before cooking. Nothing is more embarrassing for a host than seeing a hair on a guest's dinner plate. And be careful if she's Scandinavian—Norwegians burn easily.

Spicy Porker Luau Style

Serves 8

I admit it—I'm a chubby chaser. Do I refer to the habit of dating overweight women? I think not. I'm

talking about chasing down a nice plump victim for dinner. Taking a five-foot-three-inch, 325-pound porker to a deserted beach, giving him a one-hundred-yard head start, and then teaming up with a few friends to run him down awakens long-suppressed genetic memories of the hunt. While this is going on, the ladies can be back at the campsite, digging the pit and collecting sticks, branches, and palm fronds for the fire.

1 gallon homemade beef stock
2 stalks lemongrass
10 ancho chile peppers
2 garlic cloves
2 12-ounce bottles Rose's lime juice
1 porker (to be considered a porker, he must have a ratio of
    4 pounds to 1 inch of height)
1 apple

Get the fire going.

Combine beef stock, lemongrass, chile peppers, garlic cloves, and 1 bottle of lime juice in a large saucepan, bring to a boil, then simmer for 20 minutes. Pour into a basting bowl.

Roast the porker for 4 hours, basting liberally every 15 minutes.

Serve with an apple in the porker's mouth.

Use the second bottle of lime juice for gimlets.

OMNIVOROUS'S HELPFUL HINT: It's always good to remind those of the Hebrew persuasion that there is a difference between pork and a porker. One is *trayf*, the other is terrific.

OMNIVOROUS'S HELPFUL HINT #2: When it comes to a meal, supersize it!

Silence of the Lamb Chops

Serves 2

A lamb is a sheep that is younger than one year old. To a cannibal, age is irrelevant. A lamb is any victim that just rolls over and gives up. Think of the 1999 Los Angeles Lakers or the French army.

Rib cage of 1 "lamb"
2 teaspoons butter
1 medium onion, diced
1 garlic clove
2 orange slices

Melt the butter and sauté the onion, garlic, and orange slices. Season the lamb with your sauté.

Roast at 375 degrees for 20 minutes.

OMNIVOROUS'S HELPFUL HINT: I recommend total quiet while cooking this. Hence, the silence of the lamb.

Steak Diana

Serves 2

It's time for a confession. Remember that unknown Fiat driver who cut off the Mercedes in the tunnel under the Seine causing Henri Paul, Dodi Fayed and Princess Di's driver, to crash? I confess, I was in the mood for steak Diana. Because of the paparazzi, it didn't work out as planned. However, if her brother, Earl Spencer, can spend the rest of his life cashing in on her fame, I can take advantage by offering you the recipe she inspired.

2 club steaks
6 teaspoons butter
2 tablespoons sherry
1 teaspoon chives
Cognac from the period of the second Napoleonic conquest

To obtain the steak, club a member of the Royal Family. Because they are English, use a cricket bat instead of your 32-inch, 27-ounce Easton. Remove the teeth and gums, as they are undoubtedly rotten and plagued by gingivitis and pyorrhea.

Sprinkle salt in a heavy skillet over medium heat. Brown the salt. Add the steaks and brown. Coat with butter, sherry, and chives.

Blaze with cognac, drink some cognac, and toast the fact that for the first time in nine hundred years a member of the Royal Family has amounted to something worthwhile.

OMNIVOROUS'S HELPFUL HINT: Remember, do not be turned away by the outward appearance of a member of any Royal Family. It's the result of too much inbreeding.

Smothered Skirt Steak

Serves 1

I start this meal by inviting a young lady over for smothered skirt steak. Imagine her surprise when she sees the table set for one.

But, gentle reader, just because you decide to suffocate a woman in a skirt doesn't mean you're a misogynist. You just might be in the mood for smothered skirt steak. In fact, just because your victim is wearing a dress doesn't even mean it's a female. Take J. Edgar Hoover. Or RuPaul. Or Gertrude Stein.

1 10-ounce flank
2 tablespoons unsalted butter
1 teaspoon garlic
1 onion
1 cup beef stock

Smother the skirt. Remove the skirt. Cut out a 10-ounce piece of flank. In a heavy skillet, melt the butter, add garlic and onion. Cook until golden.

In a second skillet, sauté the flank. Pour the beef stock onto the onion-garlic sauté, heat, and pour over the flank.

OMNIVOROUS'S HELPFUL HINT: This is the perfect meal for a dinner date. Or for a perfect date dinner.

New Guinea Father's Day Brains

Serves 1

This recipe was brought to the public's attention in 1992, when anthropologists discovered a number of cannibal tribes in the remote jungles of Papua New Guinea. It was the custom of the father of a newborn in their tribe to celebrate the birth by killing a man he knew who had the same name as he'd given the child, taking the brain and eating it. Talk about zero population growth!

As a cannibal, you don't want to wait for the birth of a newborn to enjoy this delicacy. Make it an annual tradition by serving it every Father's Day. It certainly beats giving the old man a necktie and another bottle of Old Spice.

Lemon juice
1 small bowl ice water
Brains

Use an eyedropper to put 5 drops of reconstituted lemon juice into the ice water. Taking a melon scoop, remove the brains of your victim. Dip in ice to solidify, then eat.

OMNIVOROUS'S HELPFUL HINT: Raw brains can occasionally cause kuru, a disease that leaves its victims in a complete vegetable state. Which means that tonight's dinner guest can become tomorrow's vegetable platter.

Short Ribs

Serves 2

Some people watch *The Wizard of Oz* for the great songs. Some watch it because Judy Garland is the diva they love. I watch it because the Munchkins always put me in the mood for short ribs.

1 can Italian plum tomatoes
4 cloves garlic
1 tablespoon parsley
Onion
Rosemary
Cinnamon
1/2 cup oil
1 rib cage of a midget
2 cups 1996 Justin Vineyards "Isosceles"

In a bowl, mix together the tomatoes, garlic, parsley, onion, rosemary, and cinnamon.

Heat the oil in a medium skillet. When hot, add the short ribs.

Pour the sauce over the ribs. Drink the wine to help with any guilt over the fact you just killed a man three feet, eight inches tall. This has never been a problem for me, but it may be for you.

OMNIVOROUS'S HELPFUL HINT: Every July, the Little People of America hold their convention in LA. It's a short ribs festival.

Boned Quayle with Currant Sauce

Serves 10

This recipe raises an interesting philosophical question for a cannibal—is Dan Quayle a bird or a vegetable? It is important to go beyond his answers to routine questions, for if one does not do that, one is led to the inescapable yet wrong conclusion that he is merely a vegetable and, therefore, *trayf* for a cannibal. But if one consults Darwin or any of the major ornithologists, one realizes he has the qualities of a vegetable *and* the three major characteristics of a bird; thus, he is edible. He (1) has a brain smaller than a walnut, (2) flies away in the face of combat, and (3) will fly into windows while gazing at his own reflection.

1 boned Quayle
3 minced shallots
4 tablespoons olive oil
¼ cup currants
Salt and pepper to taste
½ quart homemade chicken stock

Sauté the bones and shallots in the olive oil over medium heat until brown. Add the bones, shallots, currants, salt, and pepper to chicken stock. Simmer.

Sauté the Quayle until golden brown; serve with currant sauce.

Note that this Quayle only has right wings.

OMNIVOROUS'S HELPFUL HINT: You can lure the Quayle out of its hiding place with the promise of NRA money.

OMNIVOROUS'S HELPFUL HINT #2: This dish is best enjoyed watching a rerun of *Murphy Brown*.

Haggis

Serves 1

My Scottish roots are showing. There is no better dish on a cold winter's night than a steaming bowl of haggis. The dish is commonly believed to be made from the entrails of a sheep stuffed with spices, kidneys, lungs, and liver. However, would a thrifty Scotsman kill one of his prize sheep so he could eat the intestines? Would a shepherd ruin the source of his wool for entrails that look, taste, and feel the same as a person's? Would a member of the Wallace clan let the death of William Wallace go unavenged for 650 years with so many annoying Englishmen around? I think not.

Entrails of an Englishman
Pepper
Onions

Catch an Englishman. Skin him. Boil him. Stuff his kidneys, livers, intestines, and lungs inside his stomach. Add pepper and onion.

Bake at 350 degrees for 30 minutes.

Serve steaming hot with a single-malt scotch.

OMNIVOROUS'S HELPFUL HINT: If you are in America and looking for an Englishman, they can be found just about anywhere except at the dentist office.

THE FOURTH COURSE

Americans believe salad should be eaten before the meal. The true gourmand knows salad is to be enjoyed *after* the main course. For those who want to keep the tradition of a fourth course without having to deal with food that is grown—and I shudder while typing these words—*under the soil,* here are four suggestions.

Mixed Greens

Serves 2

Find two environmentalists at a Green Party rally. Toss them in a blender and serve them garnished with some unread leaflets. It's the ultimate in recycling.

Cauliflower Ears in a Honey-Mustard Sauce

Serves 4

Boxing is more than the sweet science. It is the world's leading supplier of cauliflower ears. These can be enjoyed as a crunchy hors d'oeuvre or, as I prefer, as a way to clean the palate after a heavy meal.

4 ounces honey
4 ounces mild Dijon
8 chilled cauliflower ears

Mix the honey and Dijon to create a dip.

Wash the cauliflower ears. Arrange in a clockwise pattern on some Bibb lettuce leaves and ice. Serve.

OMNIVOROUS'S HELPFUL HINT: I have two words for people who don't think this tasty treat can fill you up—Prince Charles.

Hearts and Palm

Serves 2

When I was sixteen, my father took me to New York City to see *Man of La Mancha.* After the play, we went to the famed Palm Restaurant. You cannot imagine the disappointment on this boy's face when he discovered that the entrées were from a cow and not actual human palms. But proving that a cannibal can find inspiration anywhere, I took the opportunity to come up with this recipe.

1 heart
2 palms

Wash, chill, and serve *au jus.*

OMNIVOROUS'S HELPFUL HINT: Remember, always wash those hands.

A Garden Salad

Serves 1

Find someone who has a green thumb. Stalk him, kill him, eat his thumbs.

NUTS

Why do cannibals finish a meal off with nuts? The same reason a dog licks them—because we can.

Sierra Nevada "Rocky Mountain" Oysters

Serves 2

This is based on the original recipe found in diaries and notebooks of the Donner Party. Their adventure of dining al fresco occurred in 1847; however, the eating of—how should I put this?—the family jewels has been practiced since the days of the caveman. Back then, the Neanderthal thought eating his rival's cookies would give him strength. Today, we know it as nice light eating. For those who still don't know what we are talking about, a joke I heard at Oxford will illustrate: Two cannibals are eating an English explorer. One has started from his head, the other from his toes. After a few minutes, the one at the north end says, "How is it going?" The one at the south end says, "I'm having a ball." The other responds, "Stop eating so fast."

6 "oysters"
1 cup 1995 Qupé Chardonnay
½ cup bread crumbs
Kosher salt
2 tablespoons butter

Soak the oysters in a cup of Chardonnay overnight. In a small mixing bowl, combine bread crumbs and kosher salt to make a coating for the oysters. Coat the oysters in the mixing bowl.

In a small saucepan, over low heat, melt the butter. Fry the oysters until they are golden brown. As women know, all men's oysters are done after 2 minutes.

OMNIVOROUS'S HELPFUL HINT: Only eat someone's oysters in an *R* month.

OMNIVOROUS'S HELPFUL HINT #2: In a pinch, if you can't find fresh ingredients, you can always root through the disposal bags at a vasectomy clinic.

Chopped Nuts

Serves 4

Do you remember the slogan "Sometimes you feel like a nut, sometimes you don't"? Let's have a pop quiz. That was:

1. The ad slogan of a candy company.
2. The legal defense I used to avoid death row.
3. Lorena Bobbitt's choice of revenge.
4. A delicious after-dinner snack.
5. All of the above.

If you feel like a nut, have some. There are two types of nuts. The first can be found in their protective casing about 8 inches south of the navel. The other type of nut can be found at any NRA convention. Either way, just chop and serve.

OMNIVOROUS'S HELPFUL HINT: If you're shopping for nuts at an NRA convention, remember, they sometimes put up a fight.

OMNIVOROUS'S HELPFUL HINT #2: There is a bar in Reading, Pennsylvania, near Albright College called the Peanut Bar where patrons are encouraged to throw the shells on the floor. Just for fun, during baseball season, salt and serve your nuts in their original shells.

Roasted Mixed Nuts

Serves 1

Nutritionists the world over praise the health value of nuts. Baseball fans love eating them at a game. But why spend $3 for a bag of stale, oversalted ballpark nuts when you can bring your own fresh ones. I find that on a hot July day, there is invariably one car in line for parking forced to pull over to the side of the road with an overheated radiator. Two things are true in this situation. (1) Everyone will be so focused on getting into the stadium that they will totally ignore anything happening on the side of the road; and (2) Triple A will take an hour to get there. That gives you about twenty minutes to harvest your nuts, bag them, and be in your seat by the bottom of the first.

OMNIVOROUS'S HELPFUL HINT: Don't forget their wieners! At least you know those are 100 percent beef. God only knows what's in a ballpark hot dog.

OMNIVOROUS'S HELPFUL HINT #2: Make sure to bag them quickly. They're much better when they're red hot.

OMNIVOROUS'S HELPFUL HINT #3: I have never met a bigoted or prejudiced cannibal. To those of us who follow the cannibal path, all men are one color—pink on the inside. That is why I always recommend mixed nuts.

WHAT I MEAN BY "FROM SOUP TO NUTS"

If the first rule of cannibalism is always to eat what you kill, the second rule is *never* to let anything go to waste. People are to cannibals what buffalo were to Native Americans—sacred animals no part of which should go to waste. Bones can be used for soup, the non-edible internal organs are perfect for beef stock, the ears and nose make a lovely garnish, fingers and toes are wonderful appetizers, and, of course, the nuts can be used for . . . nuts.

4

VEGETABLES AND DESSERTS

A MEDICAL MINUTE

While in England — and, no, I will not give any persistent Interpol agents any details that could help them track me down — I spent some time working for Lloyd's of London. Did you know that every year, twelve thousand people in the British Isles are taken to the emergency ward for inserting a vegetable into a body orifice? This is the problem with the English—they boil their meat and shag their vegetables.

ABOUT VEGETABLES

As Dr. Barry Sears pointed out in his groundbreaking book *The Zone,* one million years ago our bodies evolved to eat and digest in a particular way; in essence, we are genetically programmed to eat protein and fat. That is why there are so many unhealthy, overweight people today—eight thousand years ago, we began to add vegetables and grains to our diet and the result is an explosion of fat.

That is the true beauty of cannibalism. As a protein and fat eater, you are getting your body fit and using it the way nature and the Supreme Being intended. And living in a world with so many grain and vegetable eaters provides us with a buffet of adipose entrées to choose from.

Remember, as a cannibal, the only vegetable you want to eat is Dan Quayle.

IF YOU HAVE THE MIDNIGHT MUNCHIES

I admit it, I have a sweet tooth. Actually two. They're from the jaw of a diabetic from Copenhagen named Ernst whom I killed by depriving him of insulin while feeding him mass quantities of raw sugar.

I then had him as my favorite dessert—Danish and coffee.

There are three other desserts that can easily be made from the simple ingredients found in your rendering sink: blood pudding, ladyfingers, and kidney pie.

5

GRILLING

First of all, let's be semantically correct—"barbecue" is not a verb. It is and has always been a noun. "Grill" is a verb, "barbecue" is a noun. Let me give you an example of improper and proper usage.

Improper: Janet Reno barbecued forty-seven Branch Davidians in Waco.

Proper: Janet Reno grilled forty-seven Branch Davidians, which made it a large Texas barbecue.

Now that we have the terminology correct, let us proceed with a brief discourse on the history of grilling. Humans have been roast-

ing each other over open flames for thousands of years. Originally, it was done for religious purposes, to wit, the roasting of the ceremonial virgin to appease the gods. That tradition slowly died out. Not the roasting part. Virginity.

Then, in the Dark Ages and the early days of the Renaissance, people were roasted to death as a means of punishment. History and Hollywood point to Joan of Arc being the prime example of this type of grilling. As far as we know, she was never eaten. Before or after death. The practice of burning people alive for entertainment as opposed to food reached its boiling point at the Salem witch trials. At that point, our Founding Fathers deemed the practice of witch trials barbaric and replaced them with the process of impeachment. At present, there are only two places in the world where people are grilled on a regular basis. First is Texas's death row; second is at Chez Omnivorous between Memorial Day and Labor Day.

PUT ANOTHER SHRIMP ON THE BARBIE

To a cannibal, Paul Hogan's "put another shrimp on the barbie" only means one thing—we're grilling short people tonight. Dwarfs, midgets, little people, leprechauns, whatever you call them, they grill up great.

I have a few tips for those who are in the mood for grilling some shrimps.

Omnivorous's Rules of the Barbecue

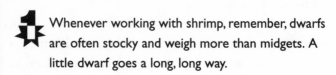

1 Whenever working with shrimp, remember, dwarfs are often stocky and weigh more than midgets. A little dwarf goes a long, long way.

2 They tend to travel in packs. So if you're out looking for one, you may end up bringing home anywhere from three to six.

3 Don't overcook. I always recommend Pittsburgh Rare.

GRILLING IN THE SOUTH

Grilling in the South has taken on an entirely new meaning since the Tennessee State Senate passed the "roadkill bill." This unique and forward-thinking piece of legislation allows motorists to take home and eat anything they hit with their car.

Of course, cannibals have been doing this for years, hidden from the public eye. Now, according to my interpretation of the roadkill bill, we can legally do it in the great state of Tennessee.

Think about it. No more hiding in the cannibal closet! No more sneaking out at 4:00 A.M. hoping to hit a drunken transient. No more "accidentally" hitting a jaywalker, claiming you're a doctor and then rushing him to your private "hospital." Now, if you're a cannibal, you can stay at the Peabody in Memphis—I always demand the presidential suite—go for a nice Sunday drive, leisurely watch the tourists visit Beale Street, pick out your entrée (it's like choosing from a lobster tank), put the pedal to the metal and, voilà, you've got dinner on the grill.

OMNIVOROUS'S SPECIAL TIP
Stop! Stop right there. I can't believe I've shared my philosophy, my recipes, my sense of history, without giving you a bit of advice my mentor cannibal* once gave me: "Always have a good dental plan."

Brush, floss, keep those pearly whites in great shape because they are the tools of the trade. Personally, I like the Delta dental plan. And use Crest. It's recommended by four out of five dentists for their patients who chew on gums.

*And, yes, there are mentor cannibals. I myself have personally taken a number of young men and women under my tutelage, teaching them at a once-a-week seminar. It was at the Learning Annex. I even give a final exam. An oral exam. The A and B students join me for dinner; the C and D students prepare the dinner. The F students are dinner.

6

CANNIBALISM FOR THOSE WITH SPECIAL NEEDS

Can anyone enjoy the cannibal lifestyle? Absolutely. Even those with "special needs."

KOSHER CANNIBALS—A SPECIAL SECTION FOR THOSE OF THE HEBREW PERSUASION

In the circles I run in, I have become acquainted with many of the Hebrew persuasion. In fact, some of my best meals have been Jewish. And it always seemed odd to me that there were so few Jewish cannibals. Then, one Sunday, while receiving Confession—I particularly like the wafer part where one partakes of the body of Christ—I began to think. Why was I put on this earth? Could it be that I am God's agent to spread the gospel of cannibalism to the Hebrews? To that end, I took it on myself to solicit questions from the Jewish community and, with the help of my friend Rabbi Harold Greenstein, have come up with a guide to help the Chosen People choose people.

Q: What special rules are there for being a kosher cannibal?
A: You have to keep two sets of dishes—dairy and meat.

Q: Are there any special prayers before the meal?
A: There is a blessing over the food. *Baruch ata adonai elohainu melech ha'olam borai pri* people.

Q: Is there any time when a Jew should not eat another person?
A: Yom Kippur.

Q: Are there any special kosher recipes?

A: Potato foreskins.

Q: What about any special rules regarding the victim?

A: A rabbi must be present at the killing to make sure it is done as humanely as possible.

Q: Isn't eating another person the worst thing a Jew could do?

A: No, that would be paying retail.

Q: Do you need to keep two sets of dishes?

A: No, two sets of teeth, one for dairy, one for meat.

Q: Can you be a Jewish cannibal anywhere?

A: Just about anywhere. Although some country clubs in the South are restricted.

NOTE: Cannibalism can be practiced by people of every religion. Even the Amish. Just as long as electricity isn't involved.

CANNIBALISM FOR THOSE ON A LOW-CALORIE DIET

It is my belief that a high-protein, high-fat diet can actually make you healthier. But I understand that there are those who cannot handle a high-calorie diet. Fortunately, there is a solution that can enable them to enjoy the benefits of cannibalism without piling up unwanted calories: Catch and eat a supermodel. The comparison below will help illustrate.

Normal 28-year-old woman: 125 pounds, approximately 300,000 calories.

Kate Moss: 78 pounds, 1,200 calories.

OMNIVOROUS'S HELPFUL HINT: If you really want to get into the supermodel lifestyle, binge, then purge.

OMNIVOROUS'S HELPFUL HINT #2: When trying to catch a supermodel, use a mirror. They are attracted to their own reflection.

CANNIBALISM FOR ANIMAL RIGHTS ACTIVISTS

How does one reconcile being a member of PETA with the desire to partake of human flesh? Is it barbaric to kill and eat a human being as opposed to eating an animal? I think not.

First of all, unlike veal or animals raised for slaughter, people are free-range. Second, unlike a harmless lamb, most people deserve what's coming to them. Finally, as a member of PETA, you can justify the killing of people as a punishment for their killing of spotted owls, minks, and desert tortoises. In short, there is no hypocrisy if a PETA member eats a human—just as long as they don't wear his fur.

7

ETHNIC FOODS

Face it, we all get tired of basic American cuisine. Who among us hasn't longed for a more exotic taste, something different on the palate. In short, cannibals, just like you, want to eat Chinese on Saturday night.

CHINESE

I spent six months touring China in 1994. Think of China not as the world's most exotic country, think of it as the world's largest buffet. One billion entrées. Chinese food tends to be a bit on the spicy side, so I recommend a nice Riesling. Remember, the old rules don't apply—you don't have to have red wine with meat.

MY FAVORITE CHINESE MEAL: Spareribs, paper-wrapped peasant, and an entrée of Young Hung Guy.

OMNIVOROUS'S HELPFUL HINT: Make sure to remove the entrails. Otherwise, you give a new meaning to "pu pu" platter.

ITALIAN

How do you make tortellini family-style? Start with the Tortellini Family. Or any of the other five families—Barzini, Tattaglia, Corleone, or Soprano. I have found the best way to find Tortellinis is in the trunk of a Lincoln on the bottom of the East River. It's a heavy meal, especially with the cement, but well worth it. *Cent'anni!*

OMNIVOROUS'S HELPFUL HINT: If asked where you got this recipe, remember, you didn't see nothing.

CENTRAL AMERICAN/MEXICAN

Sadly, the pioneering work in the field of early cannibal cooking by the Inca and Aztecs was lost when they were wiped out by disease and the conquistadors. Yet, there is a reason those two civilizations have long been considered among the most advanced in the world—they believed in cannibalism.

Although these great recipes have been lost forever, I for one am particularly fond of basic Latino cuisine. But forget the wine—when eating the delicacies of that region, every cannibal knows the way to go is with *mas cerveza.* The best place to find a meal is along the banks of the Rio Grande on a moonless night. Not only can you find yourself a great meal, you are bringing a smile to the face of Pat Buchanan.

JAPANESE

The Japanese are masters of three things—electronic engineering, surprise attacks, and the art of the "presentation chef." The performance skills of the legendary Benihana cooks are impressive, but not nearly as impressive as the ginsu knifework of the cannibal Japanese chefs.

One of the great nights in my life was spent in the back room of a small restaurant in Yokohama watching Japan's most famous samurai chef dice and slice a sailor right at our table, flipping choice parts onto the grill and into our mouths. I have never tasted more delicious beef. Was it the presentation that made the night so exotic and special, or was the fact that the sailor was drunk the key? Perhaps the latter. For if rubbing with gin and feeding their prize Kobe cattle mass quantities of beer make them more tender, perhaps the same works with their prize human beef.

OMNIVOROUS'S HELPFUL HINT: It is important to bow to the chef when he is done with his presentation. However, do not bow too low; he may think you are offering him his next entrée.

8

HOLIDAY DINING

Everyone has a favorite memory of a holiday get-together with their loved ones. Mine was Christmas of 1956. We were all sitting around watching the Lionel Barrymore version of Dickens's *A Christmas Carol.* My grandmother was weeping at the plight of the poor Cratchit family; I, of course, sympathized with Scrooge. As I was explaining to "Nana" why I felt a kinship with Ebenezer, I realized it wasn't that I liked him, it was just that I couldn't comprehend how the Cratchits could be hungry while living amidst plenty. Their solution was right before their eyes. Tiny Tim! He was dying anyway. At eighteen pounds, he was the perfect size to feed a family of eight. Plus, his no-longer-needed wooden crutch could be thrown on the fire to make the house warmer. I could never understand how people can go hungry in a buffet. The late, great Sam Kinison once said that instead of sending the starving people in the Sahara food, we should send them U-Hauls so they could pack up and move out of the desert. I think Sam didn't go far enough. Wherever there are starving people, we should send them a recipe book and a filleting knife.

Here are some tips on cooking for the Big Three holidays: Thanksgiving, Christmas, and Día de los Muertos (Day of the Dead).

Thanksgiving

There is nothing more frightening in a young wife's life than the first time she has her in-laws over for Thanksgiving dinner. For a cannibal, having the in-laws over for dinner the first time is also the last time. I will skip the usual borscht belt comedian's jokes about how tough one's mother-in-law is; the truth is, after a day of basting and long, slow cooking, this tough old bird is as tender as they get.

Make sure that your in-laws are free from bruises. Also, before stuffing, make sure the cavity has a fresh, clean smell. When in doubt, throw the in-law out!

OMNIVOROUS'S HELPFUL HINT: The best part about having both in-laws—4 drumsticks.

OMNIVOROUS'S HELPFUL HINT #2: The second best part about having in-laws for dinner—plenty of white meat.

OMNIVOROUS'S HELPFUL HINT #3: The next best thing about having in-laws over for Thanksgiving dinner—no more in-laws.

THE CANNIBAL LOVER'S COOKBOOK

Baked Christmas Hams with Pineapple and Bourbon

Serves 12

The tastiest parts of the human body are the "hams." And hams are at their plumpest and juiciest in December, after they've started to put on the post-Thanksgiving holiday fat. And who has the best hams? Our friend the plumber.

At the first sign of a winter freeze, walk a block from a plumber's shop (don't call, you don't want to leave a traceable phone record, and don't walk in, you don't want eyewitnesses). Flag down the plumber as he's going to an appointment. Slip him $100 cash to immediately take care of your frozen water pipe. When he gets to your house, watch him as he bends over. Ask yourself: Are the hams large and firm, are they plump and ripe, can I find a better meal than these two hams staring me in the face? I think not.

2 large hams (12 to 14 pounds)
Cloves
1 cup dark brown sugar
6 cans pineapple chunks
2 bottles Wild Turkey 101 bourbon

Peel the skin from the hams. Score the fat in a diamond pattern and insert cloves. Place brown sugar evenly over the hams.

Bake 30 minutes at 350 degrees. Pour pineapple over them. Cook until internal temperature is 140 degrees. With hams, always use a rectal thermometer.

OMNIVOROUS'S HELPFUL HINT: Save the skin and bones for delicious hambone soup.

Día de los Muertos

Día de los Muertos, the Day of the Dead—how does that old song go: "It's the most wonderful time of the year"? The actual holiday is of Mexican origin and is used to honor those family members who have passed on. Is there a better way to honor the dead than a good old-fashioned "family dinner"? And is there a better way to teach the fine young cannibals in your family about the importance of tradition than by gathering around and gnawing on a bit of great-grandfather? I think not.

For longtime cannibal families, the ritual involves bringing great-grandfather from the freezer, thawing out a small piece and, much like those of the Hebrew persuasion with their Passover afikomen, hiding one of the bones for the children to find. Remember, there are 206 bones in the human body, plenty for decades of Días de los Muertos fun.

For new converts, the most important part of this holiday is choosing which family member to slaughter. I believe it is up to the male head of the household to choose the most annoying member of the family, but, then again, I believe in a patriarchal society. For those who are more modern, let everyone vote.

And one reminder—kids love playing with the wishbone!

A SPECIAL NOTE ABOUT HOLIDAY DINING ON A TIGHT BUDGET

Thankfully, these are good economic times. But not all families are able to share in the economic boom of the past few years. There are those who wish to enjoy the cannibal lifestyle but are worried about the cost. They should fear not—for there is a simple way a lower-middle-class family can enjoy the cannibal life at holiday time.

You don't have to be Einstein or Omnivorous to figure this out. Admittedly, and with no modesty whatsoever, I am one of the leading intellectuals of our time. In short, I have a good head on my shoulders (and have had quite a few in my digestive system). But even commoners like yourself should be able to answer this question: How do you hold an Easter dinner for a family of six on a fixed income? Simple—eat one!

But, believe it or not, there are cannibals who refuse to eat their own family members. Why? What's the downside? Eating a family member is the single most effective way of ending sibling rivalry. Even the master himself, Monsieur Freud, was unable to stop brothers from fighting. But you as a cannibal can. Why spend thousands for years of unproductive therapy to resolve family issues when the problem can be solved with some fine cost-effective holiday dining?

9

A SPECIAL SECTION ON AIRLINE FOOD

I hate to fly. Cramped spaces remind me of my time in detention. Even worse, the food on airlines is terrible. Vegetable lasagna, chicken à la king, what they call a fillet— none of it is edible. However, there is one time when you can eat magnificent airline food—in the event of a plane crash.

The most famous cannibal airline meal involved the crash of the Uruguay rugby team in the Andes in 1972. Freezing, snow-blind, search abandoned, hope gone, those sixteen survivors managed to turn a negative experience into one of the great cannibal feasts in history. Let us review the mechanics of a plane crash to understand why airline food can be such a delicacy.

1 As the plane plummets to the ground, your brain sends a message to the adrenal gland to pump out massive quantities of hormones. Blood pressure rises, the liver pours out glucose. In short, the body is tenderizing itself and sweetening the meat.

2 Airline victims tend to be charbroiled or, as the Pentagon would call them, MREs—meals ready to eat.

3 The more you fly, the greater your risk of crashing. Conversely, those who crash tend to be frequent airline passengers who spend a lot of time sitting in a cramped space, thereby increasing their percentage of marbleized fat.

CONCLUSION: With luck, you can get a charbroiled marbleized rump roast with a caramelized crust from any frequent flier.

I know what you're thinking: "If I'm on that flight, I might not survive." To enjoy a tasty airline meal, PLEASE do not limit your thinking. Airline food can be enjoyed by nonfliers with a bit of ingenuity. True, these meals are not planned, but the true cannibal considers a plane crash a spontaneous potluck dinner.

What I recommend is turning on CNN every few hours to see if there has been a land-based plane crash. If there is one within a few hours' flying or driving time, immediately hop in your car or book a flight to the scene. (Note that I do not call it a "disaster" scene—would one call a buffet a disaster?) Don't worry, seats will be available on any flight to the site of the crash because, for some inexplicable reason, nearby death tends to spook fliers. The minute you get there, put on a yellow jumpsuit, plaster a red light on your rental car, and wear a badge that identifies you as being with the United Nations Hazardous Medical Waste and Body Identification Team. Local and FAA officials will leave you alone and, if asked, claim that as a UN observer, you are checking for remains of any foreign passengers. Tell them you are from Luxembourg. Nobody knows where the hell that is or has ever been there so there is little chance you will be asked probing questions. To complete the picture, hold an unlit cigarette in an affected European way. Since Americans are xenophobic, they will let you wander through the wreckage with your Hefty bag. Not only that, claiming you are a UN official stops you from getting a parking ticket.

Using your flashlight, look for people still strapped

in their seats. With any luck, you will find a completely caramelized charbroiled rump roast ready for the taking. Fill your Hefty bag to your heart's content—but, remember, your eyes are bigger than his stomach—seal the bag, place it in your car on dry ice, red-tag it with the words "Hazardous Medical Waste," ship it to your drop box (or put it on Amtrak, they'll ship it if they think it's hazardous nuclear waste), and start thinking of what kind of wine goes best with the passenger in seat 3C.

OMNIVOROUS'S HELPFUL HINT: Call me a Francophile, but I have always found that Air France has the best airline food.

10
THE BEST MEAL I EVER HAD

Few people know this, but there are cannibal restaurants. Like speakeasies during the Prohibition days,* these restaurants are open only to those in the know. I had this meal at a New York City private Cannibal Club in the spring of 1992. It was a prix fixe meal: $2,000.

---

*I consider the current crop of laws making cannibalism illegal an affront to the First Amendment and as discriminatory and unenforceable as Prohibition. I am hopeful to live to see the day when cannibals have their own Twenty-first Amendment.

Here is the menu.

APPETIZERS
Liver Patty
A succulent slice of liver from a DMV worker named Patty served in a shiitake cream sauce.
WINE: 1921 Château d'Yquem

Oysters Michael Rockefeller
Oysters from the one part of the Rockefeller heir that the rain forest tribe did not eat.
WINE: 1989 Haut-Brion

MAIN COURSE
Fillet of Plumber
This simple but classic cut of American meat was obtained at the 1991 New York City Plumbers' Convention, dry-aged for six weeks, and served, as all great steaks are, with a baked potato (eyes removed).
WINE: 1990 Dominus

SALAD COURSE
Hearts and Palms

The small yet tasty hearts and sweaty palms of three Amway salesmen, served with a raspberry vinaigrette dressing, made an excellent fourth course. The proprietor of the restaurant, whom I shall refer to as X, told me he had worried that he was going to have the heart of only one Amway representative, but, fortunately, in the Amway tradition, the salesman had a friend who had a friend.

DESSERT COURSE
Kidney Pie

Fresh-cut and steaming hot from a dialysis patient, this was served au naturel, urethra detached.

Ladyfingers

Luck was a lady that night and so was dessert.

AFTER-DINNER WINE: 1970 Fonseca

11

HOME ENTERTAINING THE CANNIBAL WAY

Much like Hugh Hefner's *Playboy* Philosophy, Omnivorous's Philosophy dictates that home entertainment should be stimulating intellectually and gastronomically. To make sure I didn't violate any rules of etiquette, I ran these suggestions by Martha Stewart. She whittled my twenty-five rules down to five basic guidelines. Although she was helpful, I have to admit, she is one really scary lady.

1 INVITE THE RIGHT NUMBER OF GUESTS.
For a home dinner party, invite the traditional biblical and satanic thirteen. Six couples and an entrée.

2 SPARE NO EXPENSE WHEN IT COMES TO WINE.
I have often said that the old rule of "Red with meat" need not apply. But whatever vintages and types of wines you choose, make sure they are worthy of your guests. The last thing you want is for people on the cannibal dinner circuit to gossip about your paltry wine selection. Remember, a cellar isn't just for torturing dinner, it's for fine wine.

3 COCKTAILS.
There is only one type of drink suitable for a cannibal cocktail party—a Bloody Mary. But, remember, go easy on the number you serve. The last thing you want is for a dinner guest to be pulled over while driving home and test positive for type O positive.

4 THE ISSUE OF SMOKERS.
Don't let smokers ruin your dinner party. If your entrée starts to smoke and burn, put his head out with a fire extinguisher.

5 THERE IS NOTHING BETTER THAN MOOD MUSIC.

Take the time and put together a good mix of songs to play on the CD. I suggest Hall and Oates's "Maneater," Streisand's "People Who Like People," Rod Stewart's "The First Cut Is the Deepest," and anything by the Fine Young Cannibals.

12
CANNIBAL
QUESTIONS

Unfortunately, the fact that there are fifteen outstanding warrants for my arrest prevents me from holding seminars to answer your questions in person. But through the very active cannibal underground or through my new Website, omnivorous@aol.com, I have been able to receive your queries. Here are answers to the questions I am frequently asked.

Q: Do you recommend cannibal cooking in a microwave?

A: Absolutely not. My philosophy is that cannibalism is for the gourmet, not for the harried housewife. Think about it—you've seen what twenty minutes in a microwave can do to a baked potato, do you want to ruin the thyroid gland of someone you took five days to stalk? I think not.

Q: I am traveling to the Continent this summer and am on a limited budget. Any suggestions?

A: Yes, I recommend a new book just on the market, *Europe on Five People a Day*.

Q: I enjoy cannibal cooking but am an extremely religious person. The Bible prohibits the taking of a life, yet I constantly crave the taste of human flesh. Is there any way I can reconcile these two things?

A: Follow my Socratic reasoning. There are people who waited in line for five weeks to get a ticket to *The Phantom Menace*. These people do not have a life. Therefore, killing and eating them is not taking a life.

Q: My doctor tells me my red blood cell count is low and I need more iron in my diet. Any suggestions?

A: Eat a steelworker.

Q: Can an Orthodox Jew practice cannibalism during Passover?

A: Since I am not of the Hebrew persuasion, I consulted with my learned friend, Dr. Harold Greenstein, on this. It is his opinion that during Passover, a member of the Hebrew faith can eat anyone they wish as long as the victim does not have a yeast infection. That would count as leavening.

Q: Do you think any of our political leaders are cannibals?
A: Not really. Although I've always wondered about Newt Gingrich. Sad to say, not one of today's political figures has shown the courage to stand up to the powerful anticannibal lobby.

Q: You're stranded on an island with one CD, one bottle of wine, and one person for company. Who and what would they be?
A: The CD would be Aaron Copland's *Fanfare for the Common Man*, the wine would be a 1970 Château d'Yquem, my dinner guest would be . . . the person who bought this book.

Q: What are your favorite movies of all time?
A: *Eating Raoul, Eyes of Laura Mars, The Man Who Came to Dinner, The Man with the Golden Arm, Goldfinger, Soylent Green, A Farewell to Arms.*

Q: As a busy cannibal "soccer mom," I don't have time to cook the kids a gourmet cannibal meal. What should I do?
A: Here's a great tip for busy cannibal moms. Use a

United States Marshal Service fifty-thousand-volt electric stun belt, the type currently being protested by Amnesty International. They're great to quickly incapacitate a victim and, if they're standing in a small pool of water, will cook and tenderize them within thirty seconds. Not only that, since the voltage is delivered just above the belt in the small of the back, it instantly prepares a steaming hot kidney pie.

Q: How can one tell whether one is in the presence of another cannibal?
A: Generally, they have incisive reasoning and strong incisors, a sharp wit, and a sharp knife. They also have a lean and hungry look about them.

Q: What about the "outing" of cannibals?
A: This is a relatively new phenomenon, the outing of cannibals on the Internet. It's a difficult issue. On one hand, I respect a person's right to privacy and their right to lead the lifestyle they choose. Not only that, it could lead to their arrest and execution, which is a terrible waste of human life and food. On the other hand, whenever a famous person is publicly identified as a cannibal, I think it helps a troubled teenager cope with "being different," knowing that they are not alone in their culinary orientation.

Q: Is cannibalism a preference or a genetic orientation?
A: Both. However, being a cannibal victim is clearly not a genetic orientation, as that gene pool tends to die out relatively quickly.

Q: I'm on a tight budget and need some tips on how to stretch a meal. Any suggestions?
A: There are two ways to stretch a meal. First is the rack. Second is a new product on the market by the people at Kraft—Cannibal Helper.

Q: What is next in your plans?
A: My goal is to open the first chain of cannibal restaurants. We'll call it Planet Cannibal. People pay $19 for a ham and Swiss at Planet Hollywood, imagine what they'll pay for a ham and real Swiss at my restaurant. We can even go one better. If the Carnegie Deli can name sandwiches after celebrities, why can't I have my own celebrity entrées? Or, better yet, open up a Carnage Deli.

Q: What is your opinion of Meals on Wheels?
A: I am 100 percent supportive. I refer not to the charity service that delivers piping-hot meals to the elderly on fixed incomes. I refer to giving a forgetful grandparent the keys to the car at night and seeing what pedestrians he can bring home.

OMNIVOROUS'S FINAL THOUGHT

Throughout this book, I have given of myself—my recipes, my outlook on life, my philosophy—as a way to repay mankind for what you have given to me—food and beverage.

Now it is time to leave you with two final thoughts. On a personal note, I hope we can meet for dinner sometime. I'll bring the wine, you bring the food. And, second, remember, for nothing is more true than this—you are what you eat.

ACKNOWLEDGMENTS

To David Rosenthal, Marysue Rucci, and all the people at Simon & Schuster who inspired and guided me through this, and who, more importantly, never demonstrated one bit of anticannibal prejudice. I owe you all a dinner.

To Jay Leno, the best boss anyone in this business could ever have.

To Jay, Billy Crystal, David Steinberg, Whoopi Goldberg, Bruce Vilanch, Pat Lee, John Moffitt, George Schlatter, Don Mischer, Lou Horvitz, Gil Cates, and Michael Seligman, all of whom gave me either a start in comedy writing or a gentle push along the way.

To Jack Dytman, Bob Myman, Les Abell, and Howard Silverstein, who take care of all the paperwork.

To James and Mary, Fang and Bridget, who have always been there for my family.

In my first book, I acknowledged at least two dozen friends; I was under the mistaken impression that they would feel compelled to go out and buy the book. Those cheap bastards expected a free signed copy. I learned my lesson. Not one of them gets a mention this time. This time I'm acknowledging a completely different group of people. And if they expect another mention in the next book, they better show up with a paid copy . . . and a receipt.

To John Romeo, whose free medical advice has kept me alive.

To Dave Boone, great writer, better friend.

To Bill Kernochan, Mark Grossman, Bob Benton, and all the people at Agoura Pony Baseball who cover for me when I'm off writing.

To the kids and parents on the Agoura Lightning baseball team.

To the LA Men's Senior Baseball Cleveland Indians baseball team (yes, for those of you who read my last book, I and my .125 batting average got traded).

To the designer of the BMW Z-3, which works as well as Viagra, plus it gives a smoother ride.

To the Kahns, the Keglevics, Mike Justice, and all the people in Agoura Youth Basketball who cover for me when I'm off writing.

To my parents; Julie's parents, Ed and Dora; Adam and Susan. Maybe next time my immediate family will actually spring for the $12 for a book.

And finally, some advice for Shaq: In foul shots and in sex, bend your knees and follow through.

ABOUT THE AUTHOR

Jon Macks is a writer for *The Tonight Show with Jay Leno.* He has also written for the Academy Awards with Billy Crystal and Whoopi Goldberg, the Emmy Awards, the American Comedy Awards, and Comic Relief. His first book, *Heaven Talks Back,* a parody of the latest spiritualism books, is considered as influential as Vatican II by a few of Jon's friends and a vast majority of Satan worshipers.

Jon was inspired to write a book about the cannibal lifestyle by the realization that after he had insulted God and all organized religions in his first book, there was little left for him to offend. More important, Jon sincerely believes that cannibalism is a lot less damaging to children than seeing nude photos of Dr. Laura Schlessinger on the Internet.

When not riding horses and fishing in Wyoming, Jon, his wife, and their three children live in Los Angeles.